However Long Forever

Companion Guide

Written by Steve & Courtney Cohen
Illustrated by Steven Cohen

However Long Forever - Companion Guide

Copyright © 2023 by Steven & Courtney Cohen

Written by: Steven & Courtney Cohen

Characters created by: Steven Cohen, Courtney Cohen,
- Reece Cohen, Shelby Cohen, and Makayla Cohen

Illustrated by: Steven Cohen

Layout by: Steven Cohen

Published by Now Found Publishing, LLC

Southlake, Texas

NowFoundPublishing.com

ISBN: 978-1-942362-28-9

All rights reserved. No part of this book may be reproduced or transmitted in any form or by any means, electronic or mechanical, including photocopying, and recording, or by and information storage and retrieval system, without permission in writing from the publisher.

Dear Parents, Teachers, Family, and Counselors
(and anyone else who is reading *However Long Forever* to a child),

We have created this guide to help you and your child process in depth the poem and illustrations you will encounter in **However Long Forever**. This book addresses real situations that your child has likely encountered. We want to equip you with questions, talking points, and a fun scavenger hunt so you and your child can get the most from **However Long Forever**. Visit http://howeverlongforever.com to purchase your copy and for more information on Omari.

Activities in this Guide Include:

- **Scavenger Hunt** – We have hidden some Easter eggs for you to find together. Though not necessarily eggs, we hope you have fun exploring the pages with your child for these stealthy items. You'll even discover characters from our other children's books.

- **Suggested Questions** – These are simply what they sound like – topics you can discuss while reading and looking at the illustrations together. You do not need to ask every question in one sitting. Feel free to ask other questions too. Consider these as springboards into purposeful and healing conversations. You can also use Prepare Your Heart, Background, and PCR Contemplations to guide you into deeper conversations and along your own healing and freedom journey.

- **Prepare Your Heart** – We want you to know what your child may feel. While these sections are not exhaustive, they do offer some suggestions to help you put yourself in their place and look at the world through their eyes. Think about times when you may have experienced these same thoughts and emotions so that you too can gain healing. In all situations, ask God what He says about you and your child's pain. Pour love and encouragement into your child as they express how they feel.

- **Background** – Here you'll discover the reasons we chose specific words or illustrations for each page.

- **PCR Contemplation** – This stands for Parent, Counselor, or Reader Contemplation. Although these are children's books, many older readers have also been profoundly impacted. Encounter ideas and concepts to think about in your own life and how your experience may affect your life and the life of this child.

Omari the orca was first introduced in ***Loved As You Are*** playfully exploring the seas. The name **Omari** means *flourishing* in Swahili. It is our hope and desire for all families to flourish and for children to springboard off their parents, becoming who God dreamt of and created them to be at the beginning of forever.

Foster care is one beautiful way to blend God's children together in this wonderful thing called *family*. And yet, like the depths of the sea, the challenges associated with foster care can seem endless, scary, and dark. But your love for your child is a light in that dark place. Even when we don't know how long it will last, fostering can create an atmosphere of rest, reunification, restoration, and rejuvenation. It is possibly the single opportunity some of God's kiddos will have to experience His love for them. Foster parents play an active and crucial part in a foster child's life. Although there are challenges, differences, vulnerabilities, and heartache, they are all worth it.

And, although you may not know where their forever will be, your love is a vital and important piece of their life.

Join **Omari** the orca as we dive deep into the underwater world of **Fambly** (Jamaican for *family*) to discover God's love, healing, and hope on the journey from place to place. With no promise of tomorrow, we want our kiddos to know we love them *However Long Forever*.

What to Expect: Like foster care, ***However Long Forever*** is fun and colorful as well as deep and challenging. The underwater regions of Fambly are full of beauty, perils, uniqueness, hope, and love.

Our family has personally experienced the beauty and challenges of foster care, which prompted us to share this book with you and the children you love. In this guide, we'll walk you through the book, page by page, to help you see the many hidden gems that can springboard helpful and healing conversations with your foster child.

Grab your copy of ***However Long Forever*** and join us for the scavenger hunt, deep questions, and guidance to help you in self-reflection.

Sincerely,

Steven & Courtney Cohen

If you need resources on how to handle these topics, please contact us at www.nowfound.org. We are not licensed counselors and do not claim to be able to provide psychological or clinical treatment or diagnoses. If a conversation triggers your child, please seek professional help. In case of emergency, please contact your local emergency services.

Prepare Your Heart

In this first Prepare Your Heart section, we want to prepare your heart not only for this book, but for foster care as a whole.

As parents, we need to develop a heart that encourages curiousity and deep discussion and welcomes questions of identity, culture, and heritage. We should welcome and not be afraid of questions like:

- Why do bad things happen?
- How do I deal with pain?
- Do I belong?
- How am I going to get through hard times?

We also want to honor the heritage our children carry. Their birthparents matter in ways that you may or may not understand, whether or not they're in the picture of day-to-day life. Only their unique comingling of DNA could produce this precious child. And, through these questions and considerations, we always want to point our children back to the original Source – God.

PCR Contemplation

In this first section for contemplation, like the above Prepare Your Heart, we hope you will contemplate on these questions about foster care in general and how you can help, whether that is fostering, supporting those who do, or introducing others to the beauty of family through fostering.

One of the most common reasons people are unwilling to foster is that they will become too attached and will be heartbroken if/when they are reunited with their family or taken away for any reason. With that, we want to pose these questions for you and those you encounter who seem interested, but hesitant.

- Which is worse: getting too attached and being hurt or refusing to attach in order to avoid pain?
- Imagine you lost everything and all connections with everyone familiar. What qualities about new places and people would help you begin to heal and feel safe?
- There is a time when all children leave our homes. Some will part for positive and healthy reasons, yet others will be in hardship. Since there is no gurantee that our biological children will leave in a positive manner, why aren't we so hesitant to welcome them into our house?
- Children are often less equipped to navigate change and trauma than adults. Are you willing to face personal pain in order to create a safe place for a child in need?

Gift Page:

Suggested Questions:
- You may want to ask your child if they want to write their name, so they feel a deeper connection when they look back on this book as they grow.

Prepare Your Heart
The icebergs throughout this book represent the hidden depth of your child – not just the depth of their pain, but the depth of who they were created to be, the depth of their character, and the depth of their soul. What you see day-to-day is simply the proverbial tip of the iceberg. It is up to you to look under the water to see who they really are and how they really feel.

Background
- You'll note on the first page an opportunity to write to whom this book is presented, who it's from, and when. This book is intended to belong to the child as they carry it through life, reminding them of who they are, where they came from, and the people who love them.

Title Page:

Suggested Questions:
- What kind of animal is that?
    - Follow-up: Your child may answer *killer whale*, but the proper name is *orca*.
- What animal family do you think orcas belong to?
    - Follow-up: They are a type of dolphin (or toothed whale).
- Why do you think they got their name killer whale?
    - Follow-up: Often this is answered in that they kill things. But did you know that, outside of captivity, there are few if any instances of an orca hurting a human? They acquired their name *whale killer* by helping humans hunt whales for food and blubber.

Prepare Your Heart
Killer whales are some of the most misunderstood animals. Their common name alone tells us that people have judged and labeled them incorrectly. Think about how your child has been mislabeled out of convenience and prejudice.

Background
Below the title, Omari the orca lays atop a floating iceberg full of hope, joy, and peace revealing that she is healed. While that is our heart for all foster children, we know that it would never happen without loving people standing in the gap, stepping in to selflessly love, serve, and care for these beautiful children.

PCR Contemplations
Take a moment and think about how you may have pre-judged the birthparents, the CPS worker, the judge, or even your child. Now ask God what He says about these people and how He can use you to bring His love into their lives.

Scripture Page

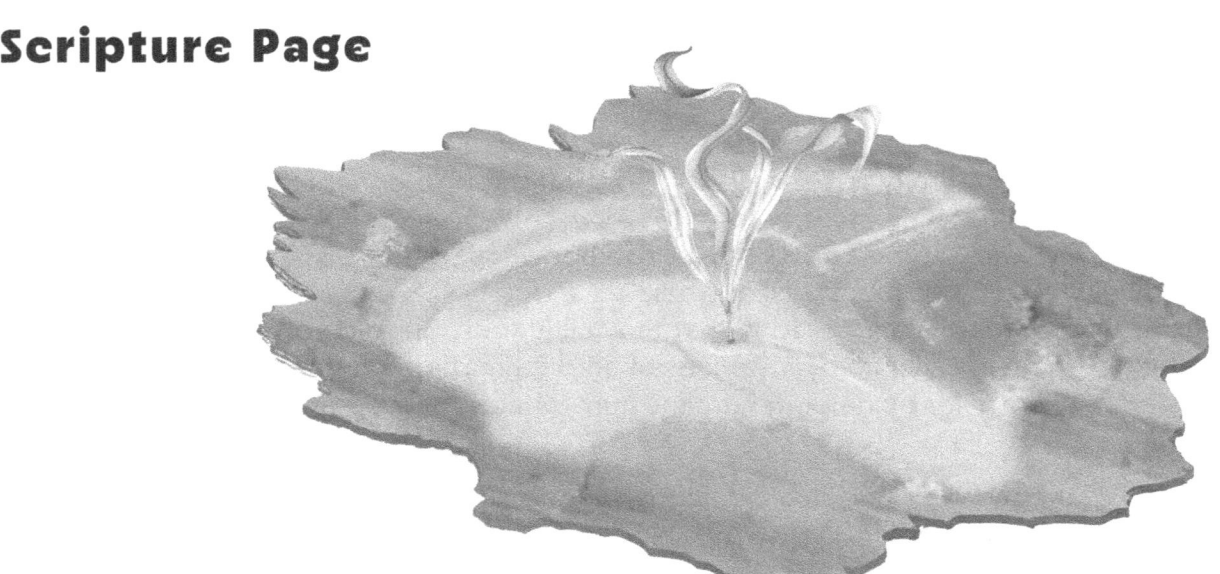

Background:
1 Corinthians 13:4-8 is a life verse for me (Steven). It speaks to what love is and isn't and what it does and doesn't do. When I was a hate-filled, atheistic anti-Christ, God showed me the number 1134 multiple times a day, almost every day. Upside down that number reads hEll, but when I asked God what it meant, He had something much more powerful and important for me. He took me to this verse to tell me He loved me. No matter how horrible I acted, no matter how far I thought I was from God, no matter how unforgivable I thought my actions and thoughts were, He loved me. We include this as the vision for this book because no matter what you have gone through, no matter what your child has done, God loves you and loves them. Let them know that today and everyday as you read this to them.

Scavenger Hunt
- How many fish can you find?
  - Answer: 27 (Some fish hide really well in the kelp, also known as seaweed). Remember that turtles are reptiles while whales and orcas are mammals. So, they don't count towards the fishy total.

Suggested Questions
- Would you rather be a turtle or a fish?
- What do you think about *family*?
  - Follow-up: Discuss why your child feels that way.
- What do you think Omari is thinking about?
  - Follow-up: How do you think Omari feels?

Prepare Your Heart

In one way or another, we've all felt lonely. Here, Omari adds to that loneliness uncertainty about the great unknown standing before her. She wonders how she can move forward in life when she has no idea where she's going. Consider stories from your life that convey a time when you felt God's presence even when it seemed like you were alone. What stories can you share with your child about how a time of uncertainty unfolded into something positive?

Background

Welcome to the land of Fambly! Our youngest daughter (who is adopted) has a Jamaican heritage, which we sought to honor in this name. We begin the story with, "When one day you wonder," because we want to give our children permission to wonder, to dream, to ask hard questions, and most importantly to see us as a safe place where they can bring all these topics. Omari is looking off in the distance, wondering where she is, where she is going, and where she belongs. She sees an endless sea in front of her – fish, turtles, and whales that all have companions – and wonders when she'll be home in her own family.

PCR Contemplation

- What part of your child's heritage can you embrace and celebrate?
- How can you help them understand why they look and sound the way they do?
- How can you honor their family even if it's difficult?

Scavenger Hunt
- What symbols of love do you see here?
- The mama dolphin is so excited she blows heart-shaped bubbles.
- There is also a treasure chest symbolizing an empty part of this family's life, just waiting to be filled.

Suggested Questions
- Would you rather live in the water or in the sky?
- What kind of treasure would you like to see fill the treasure chest?
- If you could be a dolphin, what could you do that would be the most fun?
- We call the dolphins, Mama & Daddy Dolphin. What would like to call us?

Prepare Your Heart

As foster parents, we're poised and eager for the phone call that just might change our lives. Every time the phone rings, we wonder if this will be the moment we've prepared for. For the child represented by that coming call, they are likely in one of the lowest, hardest, most uncertain moments of their young life. Everything comfortable is being shaken loose. Keeping our hearts open to love them fully and our thoughts sensitive to their tenderness and pain will be a huge help in getting through those early days and beyond.

Background

In this scene, you'll see two Spinner dolphins in their underwater home, excited to receive the sonar call from the whale in the distance. The whale represents a social worker calling the foster family with news of a coming child. We chose Spinner dolphins intentionally since dolphins and orcas come from the same species. They even share similar markings on their bodies with the orca, though their sizes are different. Our dolphins also call a sunken ship their home. Love, hope, restoration, and joy can still be found in situations or locations that may seem hopeless or lost. If you look in the lower left corner, you'll see an empty treasure chest. Their real treasure – the coming child – is on the way and this represents how they've prepared and made room in their home and hearts.

PCR Contemplation

- How can you change your attitude, actions, and surroundings to make your child feel like they are your missing treasure?
- Keep in mind that telling your foster child you have been praying for them to come to you could indeed sound like you have been praying for them to be ripped away from their family for your own self-gratification. How can you adapt your viewpoint and words to be sensitive to that possibility?
- As you look at the beauty of the shipwreck, consider the beauty of the birthparents. Even in their brokenness, they are still a treasure in the eyes of their children and their Creator. How can you help them be restored?

Scavenger Hunt
- Can you trace Omari's travels?
- Do you notice anything that changes about Omari as she travels?

Suggested Questions
- Would you rather hunt for treasure or hide your treasure?
- What do you think happened to Omari's fin?
- Have you ever felt like something broke in you?
- What do you think happened to the map to make it look the way it does?
- What do you think is missing from that torn area in the middle?
- Where have you been that is the most special?
- Where is the farthest away place you have been?
- If you could go anywhere in the world, where would you go?
    - Be prepared that your child may respond with, "Home." That is a beautiful thing to desire.
- How do you think Omari felt at each place we see her on the map?

Prepare Your Heart

This is perhaps the most poignant scene of the book – the map of Omari's journey. When a foster child enters our home, we're given pieces of their story in files, snippets of texts and conversations, pictures they may bring, and perhaps little stories they eventually share in no particular order. It becomes like a map showing us where they've been and what they've gone through. But there will often be holes in the map, those times and situations that we will never truly understand, and places of wounding. If you have biological children, you can see right away the difference in this beginning to your parenting journey and what it's like to be the primary witness to your child's life. Your biological child probably knows that you know them inside and out and love them unconditionally. Your foster child likely has arrived at your home with no such confidence.

Background

On the right side of the page, you can see the land of Fambly which Omari swims around. If you look at Omari right above the land, take note that her dorsal fin stands up straight. She's near her family and has some sense of normality. Follow the dotted line around to the middle of the spread and you'll see a tear in the map. We aren't exactly sure where Omari emerges from this hole, but notice how her dorsal fin is broken and slumped over. In nature, when an orca's dorsal fin is broken, it is impossible to repair. This break often happens when an orca goes into captivity due to the trauma of being removed from their home. (Pay attention to the fin later in the story!) Other parts of the map include the shipwreck (which happens to be where the dolphins live) and the swirling vortex in the upper left which represents a chaotic time or situation.

PCR Contemplation

- When we are sad or experiencing various emotions, there is nothing wrong with the emotion. It is an indicator that something is or isn't as expected. Emotions don't need to define us. They can simply remind us to slow down and pay attention.
- What difficult emotion do you most commonly struggle with? What do you think it may be pointing to in your life that you need help with?

Ripples In The Shallows

You came to our home
With no forever promise
Though we're unsure of how long
We love you regardless

Scavenger Hunt
- How many spots are on the sting ray?
    - Answer: 24
- Count how many coral tubes there are.
    - Answer: 55 (Don't miss the coral hiding in the distant shadows.)

Suggested Questions
- Would you rather be a lone stingray or a fish in a school?
- What do you think created the ripples in the sand?
    - How does it make you feel when something you work on gets messed up?
- Why do you think schools of fish travel in groups like that?
    - Do you feel more comfortable in groups or by yourself?

Prepare Your Heart

Behavior can seemingly turn on a dime for a child who's come from hard places. Even when things look peaceful or tranquil on the surface, know that there are currents moving beneath. Curiosity can war with feelings of betrayal causing internal friction if they show interest in something new. Prepare yourself to expect the unexpected so that you can bring empathy and understanding to your child, especially in those tumultuous moments.

Background

In this spread, we see Omari looking around her tropical surroundings in the shallower water. She sees the colorful stingray and watches with curiosity this creature that's so different from her. The sand ripples on the sea floor are caused by under currents and hydrothermal vents bubbling up from below. In the distance, schools of unidentified fish gather in community for connection and protection. We may think we can identify the fish in the distance, but until they come close, we can't be certain.

PCR Contemplation

- Think about what drives you, inspires you, and motivates you to be who you are and do what you do. What if all those things were all taken away?
- Now think about how your child could be feeling. What if the things that drive and motivate them are distrust, hurt, a feeling of not belonging, and never being home? Would you look to others for help? How might you feel about the people around you? Do you think you would trust the people that you were forced to stay with or those making those placement decisions?
- Having community around you is vital to support you in times of need, provide safety in times of peril, challenge you when you may have become complacent, pray for you continually, and be a part of all aspects of your life. What does your child's community look like right now and how can you help bring it to a healthy place?

Comfort In The Cave

Scavenger Hunt
- How many tentacles are on the octopus?
    - Answer: 9 (making our octopus an enneapus.)

Suggested Questions
- Would you rather glow in the dark or be invisible?
- What is Omari frightened of?
    - Answer: A Giant Pacific Red Octopus.
- Why do you think Omari may be afraid of the octopus?
- What do you think octopi eat?
    - Answer: Predominantly shellfish and the occasional, rare seabird.
- Why do you think mama dolphin looks angry?
    - Take this time to talk about how important your kiddo is and how deeply you take the responsibility of protecting them.
- What is daddy dolphin doing?
- How would you feel if you were Omari with a mama and daddy like this?
    - What can we do to make you feel safe in our home?

Prepare Your Heart

Love is so much more than warm, fuzzy feelings; it's also found in safety and providing a secure place. As foster parents, we are primary advocates for our children. Your child may have never felt safe. They may have never had someone advocate for their safety in a way they positively interpreted. Let's consider as many ways as we can to provide and reveal safety to our kids.

Background

This scene is darker, portraying a potential enemy (the giant, red octopus) at the door. We see Omari with fear-filled eyes being comforted by her foster dad while her foster mom keeps close watch. They both make sure that no additional harm comes to this child who has already faced so much difficulty. Nighttime can often be filled with extra challenges when fears bubble to the surface. The dolphins take their love and protection of Omari seriously no matter what time of day it is.

PCR Contemplation

- What do you know about your child? Perhaps even more important: what do they know about you? To build a safe space it may be beneficial to build common ground or to share vulnerably with them both fulfilled and dashed dreams, hopes, and desires. It's not a competition nor comparison but should be looked at as an opportunity for connection. Knowing that you have been waiting, dreaming for them may bring comfort, but be aware that it may also come across that you hope they would be ripped from their family or experience horrible trauma just to fulfill your desires. Depending on the situation and beliefs of your child, it could also come across as if God prefers you over them, because He is fulfilling your dreams and desires, at the expense of theirs, especially if their wounds are still very recent.
- Similar to orcas, octopi (the plural of octopus) are often misunderstood animals. They are masters of disguise, blending in with their surroundings, rarely able to simply and safely be. How can you create that safe place for your child to be who they were created to be?

A Shiny, Fun Flipping Day

We know you may feel
As if you don't fit in,
But I assure you we're more alike
Than you can imagine.

Scavenger Hunt
- Can you find an animal on this page that cannot swim?
    - Answer: There isn't one. Fun Fact: sea gulls can hold their breath and swim underwater to catch fish and kangaroos use their powerful hind legs and tail to powerfully swim through the water.

Suggested Questions
- Would you rather spin or do flips?
- How would you feel if you could swim so fast you could jump out of the water?
- What things do you like to do that we could do with you?
- What is your favorite part of the picture?
- Have you ever dreamt about family?
    - What did your family look like in your dreams?
    - What sort of things did you do together?
    - Where did you live and go with each other?
    - Where did you go on vacation?

Prepare Your Heart

Similarities are often difficult to find in new relationships. So often the feeling of isolation, awkwardness, or that you just don't fit in can rule our foster children's emotions. They are tasked with adapting to family after family, lifestyle after lifestyle, and it is tremendously hard for them to feel like they belong, like they fit in. We need to find ways, like a fun play day at a park, the beach, or simply in the backyard, to allow them the space to realize that we are more alike than they can imagine. Be silly with them, get on their level, and let them shine.

Background

In this beautiful spread, we see the waterfall and peaks of Fambly in the background as well as Omari enjoying time with her foster parents. They leap and spin and splash. This scene shows the greater similarities between the orca and dolphins – they all love to play in the water. Their bodies are designed to speed through water, leap, and spin in the air. To the right, on the distant shore, you'll be introduced to a new character, *Stripes*, whom we'll reveal in *Similarly Unique (coming soon)*!

PCR Contemplation

- What do you enjoy doing? What are you unwilling to do that might be the key to connecting with your child? What if truly connecting meant that you would need to play a video game, go to a skate park, or play basketball? What dreams could you fulfill by getting on the same level as your child, even if it's outside of your comfort zone?
- Although you may be from different places, families, cultures, and religions, how can you be purposeful to find the similarities? How can you make your foster child feel like they belong before they buy in or believe what you do?
- Even if your child has a different theological belief system, you can find commonalities in desires and beliefs. It may take research into what they believe to be able to understand why they believe and have genuinely caring truth-filled conversations.

Scavenger Hunt
- How many orcas can you find? (There are 20 orcas total in this picture.)

Suggested Questions
- Would you rather draw or take pictures?
- What kind of lamp is shining light on their map?
    - Answer: It's a bioluminescent sea anemone. They create their own light.
    - Follow-up: Have you ever felt that you were in a dark place and you had to make your own light?
- What is your favorite memory that you don't have a picture of?
- Why are your memories important?
- Would you like me to help you put your pictures in a special book or frame?
- Would you like us to put any of your pictures up around this house? If so, where?

Prepare Your Heart

Photos are a powerful portal to our past. They evoke emotions, revive and keep alive memories of those we love most, and invite others into moments of our life they might never be able to imagine. Often our foster children arrive with their entire life sealed in trash bags, loose photos scattered throughout. One of the best ways to connect and learn about our foster children is to take time to journey with them through their photos and life stories (and maybe we can help organize along the way). Let's be willing to allow them to share what the photos mean to them and how their photos make them feel. This is a time that allows us to speak love and life over those who mean the most to them. Telling them how beautiful their parents and siblings are and affirming their emotions over missing friends and family may be the only connection you have with them for a while.

Background

In this scene, Omari and her foster parents spend time looking at Omari's old pictures. She has lived so many moments before arriving at the dolphins' home. One of the ways they work to create a safe environment and develop connection with Omari is to discuss her stories through pictures.

PCR Contemplation

- It's normal for foster children to feel like they don't belong. As we ask these questions, we must expect answers that may be difficult to hear. But consider that if it is hard to hear, how much harder it is for your child to share, and, even more, to experience.
- Keep in mind that your child has lived many moments before they arrived at your door. As we blend ourselves together into one family – however long that may be – listening to their stories, sharing their pictures, and inviting them to reveal whatever they're comfortable sharing about their past is like standing on holy ground. It is a precious thing to grow trust.

Longing For Home

FOR HOWEVER LONG YOU'RE WITH US
A DAY, A MONTH, A LIFETIME
WE PRAY FOR HEALING AND RESTORATION
ALL TO HAPPEN IN GOD'S TIME.

Scavenger Hunt
- How many birds are on this page?
    - Answer 47 (1 – pelican, 1 – seagull on the rock, 15 – seagulls in the distance, 30 – seagulls on the closer cliffs)

Suggested Questions
- Would you rather fly or swim?
- What kind of animals are on the rock?
    - Answer: seagull and sea lion
- What do you think is special about the sea lion?
    - Maybe you've heard of Jesus being called the "Lion of Judah." In this underwater world, we like to use the sea lion to call your attention to God's love for you found in John 3:16, "that God so loved the world that He gave His only son." May the "Sea Lion of Judah" help you remember that Jesus loves you.

Prepare Your Heart

This may be one of the more challenging scenes to process. Deep down in the hearts of almost all foster children, there is a desire for reunification. It truly is the best thing for kiddos, in most situations, even when their biological family situation may not seem ideal. While adoption is a beautiful unification, reunification and restoration of God's children within their biological family is the pinnacle. As foster parents, it can feel soul crushing to hear that the child we care for wants to be with someone else. This is where the empathy rubber hits the road. We need to prioritize seeing the situation not from our vantage point, through our paradigm, but through theirs. We need to love them right where they are, sacrificing our own feelings and desires. We also must be ready to deal with the continual heartbreak after every visit, call, or court date. Our kiddos' hope gets built up so much and then is often ripped from their soul repeatedly at no fault of their own. We need to be there every time, asking God what He wants to say to His child and how He wants to show them He loves them. Lastly, keep in mind that in many cases (though not all) the family is just as crushed at not being able to be united with their child. How would you feel if your children were ripped away from you? Birthparents need your prayers and support just like their children do.

Background

In *Where Your Beginning Began* and *Loved As You Are*, we are introduced to the image of God as a Lion, representing the *Lion of Judah*. Even though this is a marine life book, we still wanted to represent God on pages where we talk about Him. We decided there may be no better way to do so than using the *Sea Lion of Judah* in the *Lion of Judah's* place.

One of our favorite travel spots is San Diego and the cliffs on the west coast. While beautiful, the cliffs, like our kiddos, are worn by waves constantly crashing into them. Like the swells of hope our children have, these waves change with the rise and fall of the tide. They change in different seasons, can be drastically different in uncertain weather, and can create chasms and gaping wounds.

PCR Contemplation

- The Bible portrays adoption as a beautiful union. God has adopted the "Gentiles" (anyone other than the Jewish people) into His family through Yeshua/Jesus, the Messiah and our Rescuer. In that adoption, God grafted these children into the same tree as His originally chosen people, the Jews. And, while adoption is a beautiful grafting, we must remember that grafting requires being removed, in many cases violently cut from something else. It is okay to remember what that old thing was, but unless that piece is connected to a life source it will die.
- If you or anyone continually pour death over your kiddo or their birth family, that is what they will receive and they will die inside. But if you pour life, honor, respect, prayer, generosity, kindness, joy, and love over your child and their birth family, they can appreciate their heritage and break free from lies and generational bondage.

A Much Needed Nap

We may not be the family you hoped for
But we will do our best
We hope in our home you will find
Peace, joy, hope, God's love, and rest.

Scavenger Hunt
- How many bubbles can you find?
    - Answer: 6
- How many dolphins do you see in this picture?
    - Answer: 4

Suggested Questions
- Would you rather sleep with your eyes open or walk with your eyes closed?
- What is Omari doing?
    - What makes you feel most relaxed?
- If you could design your own bed what would it look like?
- What makes that design special to you?
- Would you rather scuba dive in a sunken ship or play in the sand on the beach above?

Prepare Your Heart

Imagine the emotional and physical toll of being ripped from everything you love and find comfort in, the stress of living with strangers in a house, living under a totally different set of rules, in a culture not your own, and with no idea how long you will be there. Moreover, you are given prescription drugs that have sedative side effects. What do you think you might do a lot? SLEEP. While this doesn't happen in all situations, we have heard countless stories where it has. It is our responsibility as parents, counselors, guardians, teachers, respite, case workers, advocates, and family to find a way to give these children rest and to restore and energize them. It is best to work as a cohesive group to find the proper and minimal amount of medication to allow them to thrive, activities that invigorate, subjects that interest, people who encourage, and a church that instills hope, joy, love, and faith in them. But, at the beginning, letting them sleep may be just what they need.

Background

Many foster parents have received their kiddos with joy and excitement just to have them flop down and fall asleep moments after arriving. Many of the medicines prescribed to our kiddos make staying awake incredibly difficult. This illustration shows that even while they may be asleep, we are watching over them, hoping and praying for them to find peace, joy, hope, love, and God's rest in our homes.

PCR Contemplation

- Have you ever experienced something that you hoped was simply a nightmare that you were going to wake up from at any moment? How did it feel when you never woke up from it and the situation persisted?
- What are some things that wear you down? Amid those things, would you expect yourself to be easily adaptable to your surroundings?
- What are your strengths and weaknesses? What is your love language? If you have not identified them, you need to so that you can work in your strengths and know how you are motivated. I would suggest to take time to do the same for your kiddos. Find out what they excel at, how they were made to thrive, and how they receive and give love so that you can encourage and better fulfill their needs.

However Long Forever

Our prayers are for healing,
A hope filled endeavor.
No matter what tomorrow brings
We're here for however long, forever...

Scavenger Hunt
- What is different about Omari?
    - Answer: The dorsal fin is healed.
- How many children are in this picture?
    - Answer: This is a trick question because we are all someone's children, but there are 7 kids, and 15 total children.

Suggested Questions
- Would you rather climb a mountain or skate on ice?
- If you could heal anything or anyone, what or who would it be?
- If you could be one of the animals in this picture, which one would it be? Why?
- If you could go anywhere in the world, where would you go?

Prepare Your Heart

We love that there is nothing too broken for God to heal – even the things that are hidden from sight and pushed down deep. As you continue to read *However Long Forever* to and over your child, we hope you will pray for their restoration, have a heart of expectation of healing over past and future emotional wounds, and for your heart to grow exponentially for their entire family.

God is the great Healer and, while there are principles, products, and practices that we can follow that may yield some results in restoring our children, without relenting our control and allowing God to do what He loves to do, it makes the healing process exponentially harder and less effective.

Be prepared to let go of what you think is going to make things better, and ask God what He wants for His children. Ask Him what they need to find hope, joy, love, peace, and most importantly Him.

Also prepare yourself to be heartbroken. The day your kiddos are reunited or taken to another home is going to be a mixture of emotions. Anger, relief, joy, and sadness account for just a few in the mixture. But dig down deep and don't let those emotions get in the way of letting your love for these kiddos shine.

Background

There are a lot of theories about why a dorsal fin on an orca will collapse. Although very rigid, they are not made of bone, but of fibrous cartilage that cannot be restored once flopped. We believe that God is a God of love, miracles, and healing, so in this last picture we show Omari's dorsal fin restored. No matter the trauma, pain, or wound we expereince, God can heal it.

We also want the colors and imagery to stir hope, dreams, desires, and evoke a feeling of love and mystery. While we do not know how long we will have a foster child, part of us will go with them and a part of them will be with us forever. The heart behind this book and this final image is that we love our children, no matter hard it is, in this current time, however long that is, and for the forever future.

PCR Contemplation

- Is there something broken in your life that you need to let go of and let God heal?
- Are you feeling anxious or resentful about the possibility of your foster child being reunified with their birth family? Think about the love that you have for your child and how that love can live for the rest of your life.
- There is still love in the midst of mourning. In all mourning processes exists the possibility of overwhelming sadness, but also incredible joy as we remember those we love. There will be a time when your child will leave your home. This may be through reunification with their birth family, but it could also be to go off to college, get married, get a job, or simply follow what they feel God is leading them towards. Since at some point they will leave, don't hold back your love. Instead, let it pour out over them however long you have them and forever more.

Dedication

Thank you for your part in this beautiful child's life. No matter how small or large your role is in loving this child, it is vitally important to their growth, fulfillment, healing, education, and satisfaction in life. Your prayers, service, generosity, and selfless love for them is not unnoticed and we are so thankful for you.

We hope you and your child enjoy *However Long Forever* as much as we do. We are praying for you! For more resources, including coloring sheets and FAQs about Now Found, please visit http://nowfound.org.

NOW FOUND
PUBLISHING

Visit
family.nowfound.org
for more
Land of Fambly
books and additional resources.